D0919360

Spain

Sue Townsend and Caroline Young

Heinemann Library
Chicago, Illinois

© 2003 Heinemann Library
a division of Reed Elsevier Inc.
Chicago, Illinois

Customer Service 888-454-2279

Visit our website at
www.heinemannlibrary.com

Designed by Jo Hinton-Malivoire and
Tinstar Design Limited (www.tinstar.co.uk)
Illustrations by Nicholas Beresford-Davies
Originated by Dot Gradations Ltd
Printed in China
by Wing King Tong

07 06 05 04 03
10 9 8 7 6 5 4 3 2 1

**Library of Congress Cataloging-in-
Publication Data**
Townsend, Sue, 1963-
Spain / Sue Townsend & Caroline Young.
p. cm. -- (A world of recipes)
Summary: Presents recipes from Spain that
reflect the ingredients and culture of the
country.
Includes bibliographical references and index.
ISBN 1-4034-0978-1
1. Cookery, Spanish--Juvenile literature. [1.
Cookery, Spanish. 2.
Food habits--Spain.] I. Young, Caroline, 1939-
II. Title.
TX723.5.S7T69 2003
641.5946--dc21
2002155857

Acknowledgments
The author and publishers are grateful to the
following for permission to reproduce
copyright material: p. 5 Corbis; all other
photographs Gareth Boden.

Cover photographs reproduced with
permission of Gareth Boden.

The publishers would like to thank Juan
Sánchez for his assistance with the preparation
of this book.

Every effort has been made to contact
copyright holders of any material reproduced
in this book. Any omissions will be rectified in
subsequent printings if notice is given to the
publisher.

Some words are shown in
bold, **like this.** You can find
out what they mean by
looking in the glossary.

Contents

Key

* easy

** medium

*** difficult

Spanish Food

Spain is famous for its sunny climate and its beaches, but most of the country is very mountainous. In the north, the Pyrenees Mountains divide Spain from France. Much of the land is covered by the *meseta*, (pronounced *meh-SEH-ta*), which means "tableland." This is a huge platform, crisscrossed by mountain ranges, and home to bears, lynxes, and eagles. The capital city, Madrid, has the highest altitude of any capital in Europe.

In the past

Many peoples have ruled Spain over the centuries, each with their own customs and cooking styles. People who lived there more than 15,000 years ago left spectacular paintings on the cave walls in Altamira, in northern Spain. Invasions came by people from north Africa and Greece, and Celts from north of the Pyrenees. The country was ruled by the Roman Empire for 400 years, and then followed centuries of rule by people from the Muslim faith, called Moors. In 1492, the states of Spain were united under the rule of the Christian King Ferdinand and Queen

▲ *A fruit and vegetable stall at Boqueria Market in Barcelona, Spain.*

Isabella. The Spanish Empire grew, based on riches sent back from the Americas by explorers called **conquistadors.** The Spanish people used the new foods the explorers brought back, such as peppers and potatoes, in their cooking—and they still do today.

Around the country

Farming in Spain is mainly done near the coasts, where the land is most **fertile.** Spanish farmers grow grains, tomatoes, oranges, lemons, vegetables, almonds, olives, and onions, **exporting** them to many other countries. Some wines come from the northern area around La Rioja. Perhaps Spain's most plentiful crop is fish, because the waters around Spain are full of fish and shellfish.

Spanish meals

So many different peoples have lived in Spain during its history that there are many cooking styles, or *cocinas.* People may visit a **tapas** bar, which serves a selection of tasty dishes to eat. An afternoon nap, called a *siesta,* might be followed by a snack called *merienda*—perhaps hot chocolate and cake. Evening meals often have many dishes and are enjoyed by the whole family.

Ingredients

tomatoes

zucchini

olive oil

peppers

asparagus

orange

onion

olives

almonds

Serrano ham

blanched almonds

cinnamon stick

saffron

chorizo

Almonds

In Spain, almonds are used to flavor cakes, cookies, and sweets. Most grocery stores sell almonds blanched (with the shell and bitter brown skin removed), flaked, **ground,** or **chopped**.

Chorizo

These spicy pork sausages come already cooked or **cured.** They are sliced and chopped, and added to some dishes for flavor. Chorizos may have slightly different ingredients in different parts of Spain.

Olive oil

Spanish cooks **fry** food and make **dressings** for salads in oil made from olives. Fresh olives are also served as a snack.

Onions

Many farmers grow onions in Spain. Spanish onions have a stronger, slightly less sweet flavor than other onions. You can use them to make the recipes in this book, if you like.

Oranges

Oranges are a very important crop in Spain. Some are bitter, and are used to make marmalade. They are called Seville oranges, because they grow around the southern city of Seville. Sweeter types grow around the city of Valencia, in the southeast. They are delicious eaten fresh, in desserts, or made into juice.

Peppers

When red, yellow, or orange peppers are cooked, they develop a sweet, smoky taste. Green peppers are unripe red peppers, and have a slightly bitter flavor. Most grocery stores sell fresh peppers.

Saffron

The yellow threads found in the center of crocus flowers are called saffron. Saffron is very expensive because it takes so long to harvest. It adds a golden yellow color and a honey-like flavor to food. You can buy it in small packets in most grocery stores.

Serrano ham

Traditionally, this ham comes from the mountainous area of northeast Spain. *Serrano* means "from the mountains" in Spanish. If you cannot find it, you can use another dry, cured ham instead, such as Parma ham, which most grocery stores sell.

Before You Start

Kitchen rules

There are a few basic rules you should always follow when you are cooking:

- Ask an adult if you can use the kitchen.
- Some cooking processes, especially those involving hot water or oil, can be dangerous. When you see this sign, take extra care or ask an adult to help.
- Wash your hands before you start.
- Wear an apron to protect your clothes.
- Be very careful when you use sharp knives.
- Never leave pan handles sticking out because you might bump into them and spill hot food.
- Use oven mitts to lift things in and out of the oven.
- Wash fruits and vegetables before you use them.
- Always wash chopping boards very well after use, especially after chopping raw meat, fish, or poultry.
- Use a separate chopping board for onions and garlic, if possible.

How long will it take?

Some of the recipes in this book are quick and easy, and some are more difficult and take longer. The stripe across the right-hand side of each recipe page tells you how long it takes to prepare a dish from start to finish. It also shows how difficult each recipe is to make: * (easy), ** (medium), or *** (difficult).

Quantities and measurements

You can see how many people each recipe will serve at the top of each right-hand page. You can multiply or divide the quantities if you want to cook for more or fewer people.

Ingredients for recipes can be measured in two ways. Imperial measurements use cups and ounces. Metric measurements use grams and milliliters.

In the recipes, you will see the following abbreviations:

tbsp = tablespoon	oz = ounce	cm = centimeter
tsp = teaspoon	lb = pound	g = gram
ml = milliliter	l = liter	in. = inch

Utensils

To cook the recipes in this book, you will need these utensils (as well as essentials, such as spoons, plates, and bowls):

- plastic or glass chopping board (easier to clean than wooden ones)
- blender or food processor
- large frying pan
- large, high-sided frying pan with lid
- 10-in. (25-cm) heavy-based non-stick frying pan
- small and large saucepans with lids
- measuring cup
- colander
- set of scales
- sharp knife
- baking sheets
- wire whisk
- pastry brush
- **tongs**
- muffin cups

 Whenever you use kitchen knives, be very careful.

Gazpacho (Cold Tomato Soup)

This dish is traditionally from southern Spain, where summers are very hot. Serve it in a bowl as a starter, or in a glass as a cool drink.

What you need

1 red pepper
1½ lbs (700 g) tomatoes
Half a cucumber
1 small onion
1 clove garlic
1 tbsp fresh parsley
1 tbsp white wine vinegar
2 tbsp olive oil
2 oz (50 g) fresh bread
   crumbs
1 slice bread

What you do

1 Cut the pepper in half, then cut each half into three strips. Throw away the seeds and stalk.

2 Lay the pepper skin side up under a broiler. **Broil** for 5 minutes, until the skin blackens. Put it into a container and **cover** it.

3 When cool, **peel** off the pepper's skin.

4 Put the tomatoes into a colander in a large bowl in the sink. Pour in just-**boiling** water and leave for 1 minute.

5 Lift the colander out. Cut a cross on the bottom of each tomato and peel off the skin.

6 Cut the tomatoes in half. Scoop the seeds into a sieve over a bowl.

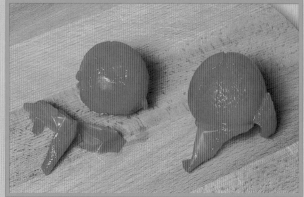

7 Put the tomatoes and pepper into a blender. Add any juice from the tomato seeds.

8 Peel the cucumber, cut off a ½-in. (1-cm) piece and put it aside. **Chop** the rest and add it to the blender.

9 Peel and finely chop the onion and garlic. Chop the parsley. Add them to the blender with the white wine vinegar, oil, and bread crumbs. **Blend** until smooth.

10 Add salt and pepper to taste. If your soup is too thick, add a little cold water. **Chill** for 2 hours.

11 Cut the crusts off the bread. Cut the bread and the leftover piece of cucumber into ½-in. (1-cm) cubes.

12 Serve in bowls **garnished** with bread cubes and cucumber.

Asparagus with Ham

In northern Spain, farmers sell their crops of green and white asparagus in local markets each spring. This delicately flavored vegetable is often made into **tapas** (see box on page 17). It makes an ideal snack or light lunch.

What you need

12 asparagus spears
6 slices dry, **cured** ham (Serrano ham, if available)
1 tbsp olive oil
Freshly **ground** black pepper

What you do

1 Trim any hard, woody pieces off the bottom of the asparagus stems.

2 Holding the asparagus in a bundle with the tips facing the same way, tap the bottoms on a board to make them level.

3 Wrap a piece of foil around the top of the asparagus. It should come two-thirds of the way down the stems.

(!) 4 Pour water into a saucepan until it is 2 in. (5 cm) deep. Stand the asparagus up in the water with the tips upwards. **Cover** and bring to a **boil**, and boil for 3 minutes.

5 Using a slotted spoon, lift the asparagus into a bowl of cold water. Take the foil off.

6 Cut the slices of ham in half lengthwise. Wrap a slice around each asparagus spear.

(!) **7** **Preheat** the broiler. Brush the ham with a little olive oil. **Broil** the asparagus for 3 minutes on each side.

8 Serve hot, sprinkled with freshly-ground black pepper.

SIESTAS

Summer afternoons are so hot in Spain that some people take a nap, called a *siesta*. Shops and cafés close, opening again in the early evening, when it is cooler.

Prawns in Batter

Spanish markets and grocery stores are full of the many different kinds of fish and shellfish caught off the coasts of Spain. This dish uses large prawns, and can be served as a **tapa** (see box on page 17) or as a starter. If you are using frozen prawns, you need to **defrost** them first.

What you need

½ tsp saffron strands (about 8)
2 oz (50 g) plain flour
Pinch of salt
½ cup (100 ml) sparkling mineral water
1 tbsp water
20 large prawns, **peeled**, but not cooked
4 tbsp olive oil

To garnish:
Sprigs of fresh flat-leaf parsley

What you do

1 Put the saffron into 1 tbsp hot water to soak.

2 Meanwhile, **sift** the flour into a bowl. Add a pinch of salt.

3 Stir in a quarter of the sparkling water to make a smooth, thick batter. Add the rest of the water a little at a time, stirring well.

4 Stir the saffron mixture. Crush the strands with a teaspoon to release the color.

5 Put a sieve over a bowl and pour the yellow liquid through it. Stir the liquid into the batter.

6 Lay the prawns onto paper towels, and pat them dry. (They need to be dry for the batter to **coat** them properly.)

! **7** Heat the oil in a frying pan. Spear each prawn with a fork or a wooden **skewer**, and dip it into the batter. Put the prawn into the pan and **fry** for 2–3 minutes, turning it over halfway through the cooking time. Fry a few prawns at a time.

8 Lift the cooked prawns onto paper towels to **drain**.

9 Serve the prawns garnished with sprigs of parsley.

Spicy Potatoes

This dish, called *patatas bravas* in Spanish, is very popular as a lunchtime snack. The potatoes are flavored with a tangy red spice called paprika, which is made from dried red peppers grown in west-central Spain. Medium-sized new potatoes are the best ones to use.

What you need

1¼ lbs (550 g) potatoes
1 tbsp olive oil
1 tbsp paprika
1 tsp ground cumin
½ tsp chili powder (if you like it)

*To **garnish**:*
Sprigs of fresh flat-leaf parsley

What you do

1 **Preheat** the oven to 375°F (190°C).

2 Wash and **peel** the potatoes. Cut into ½-in. (1-cm) chunks.

3 Put the potato chunks into a pan, add a pinch of salt, and cover them with hot water. Bring the water to a **boil**, and boil for 3 minutes.

4 Carefully **drain** the potatoes, and put them into a bowl.

5 Add the oil, paprika, cumin, chili powder, and a pinch of salt to the potatoes. Gently stir the potatoes so that you **coat** them with the spices but do not break the chunks. Spoon the potatoes into a roasting pan.

6 Cook the potatoes in the oven for 20 minutes, or until they feel soft when you stick the end of a fork into them.

7 Spoon the potatoes into a serving dish. Serve hot or cold, garnished with parsley.

TAPAS BARS

In Spain, **tapas** bars offer a wide choice of different tapas dishes, usually served in small portions. People can choose just one dish to have with a cold drink or coffee, a few to eat as a light lunch, or they can share a larger selection of tapas with friends.

Zucchini and Eggplant Fritters

Spanish farmers **export** many different vegetables to other countries. This dish is from the Balearic Islands (a Spanish province) of Ibiza, Majorca, and Menorca. It is ideal as a **tapa** (see box on page 17), or as a side dish. Spanish cooks may dip the yellow flowers of the zucchini plant in batter and cook them as well.

What you need

2 oz (50 g) plain flour
Pinch of salt
1 egg
½ cup (100 ml) milk
2 zucchinis
1 eggplant
4 tbsp olive oil

What you do

1 **Sift** the flour and a pinch of salt into a bowl.

2 Lightly **beat** the egg with a fork. Stir in the milk.

3 Add the milk mixture to the flour. **Whisk** with a wire whisk to make a smooth batter.

4 Trim both ends off the zucchinis and eggplant. **Slice** the zucchini into ½-in (1-cm) slices.

5 Cut the eggplant into ½-in. (1-cm) slices. If the eggplant is large, lay the slices flat and cut them in half again.

6 **Preheat** the oven to 325°F (170°C).

⚠ 7 Heat half the oil in a frying pan over medium heat. Using a fork, dip a vegetable slice into the batter. Let the excess batter drip off before putting the vegetable slice into the frying pan.

8 **Fry** for 2 minutes on each side, until the slices are golden brown. You can cook several slices at the same time.

9 Put foil on a baking sheet. Lift each slice onto the baking sheet, and keep warm in the oven while you fry the rest.

10 Serve hot, sprinkled with salt and pepper.

Paella (Rice, Chicken, and Shrimp)

Paella is probably Spain's most famous dish. It is not easy to make, so you will need adult help. In Spain, what goes into a paella varies according to what is available, or traditional, in different areas. Paella recipes can be passed down through generations of a family. Try this version, then experiment.

What you need

8 oz (225 g) fresh mussels (cook them on the day you buy them)
2 chicken stock cubes
½ tsp saffron strands
2 tbsp olive oil
4 chicken leg portions, cut in half
1 large onion
2 cloves garlic
3½ cups (825 ml) water
8 oz (225 g) paella rice or short grain rice
4 tomatoes
4 oz (100 g) chorizo sausages
5 oz (150 g) frozen peas
6 oz (170 g) **peeled** shrimp, **defrosted** if frozen
Lemon wedges

What you do

1 Put the mussels into clean water. Scrub each one, pulling off any feathery pieces. Throw away any that have cracked or slightly-open shells.

2 Fill a pan with **boiling** water and add the mussels. **Cover** and cook over high heat for 5 minutes.

3 Pour the mussels into a colander. Throw away any that have closed shells.

4 Crumble the stock cubes into 3½ cups (825 ml) of hot water. Stir in the saffron.

5 Heat the oil in a large, high-sided non-stick frying pan over medium to high heat. **Fry** the chicken pieces for 4–5 minutes on each side.

6 Cover the pan and cook the chicken over medium heat for 10 minutes. Carefully lift the chicken onto a plate.

7 **Peel** and **chop** the onion and garlic finely. Put them and the rice into the pan. **Stir-fry** for 3 minutes, until the rice becomes see-through.

8 Stir in a quarter of the stock. Bring to a boil, add the chicken and the rest of the stock, and boil again. Cover and **simmer** for 10 minutes, stirring occasionally.

9 Cut the tomatoes into quarters. Cut the chorizo into ½-in. (1-cm) chunks or **slices**.

10 Stir the tomatoes, chorizo, peas, shrimp, and mussels into the pan. Add a little more hot water if needed. Cover and simmer for 10 minutes.

11 Spoon the paella into a serving dish. **Garnish** with lemon wedges and serve.

21

Pork Fillet with Almonds

This recipe is from Jerez in southwest Spain, an area famous for producing a strong, sweet wine called sherry. Serve the recipe as a main dish, with potatoes or rice, and a selection of vegetables.

What you need

½ cup (50 g) blanched almonds

2 lbs (1000 g) pork fillet

1 onion

2 tbsp olive oil

1 tbsp sherry vinegar or white wine vinegar

1 pork or vegetable stock cube

2 tsp cornstarch

⅔ cup (142 ml) cream

1¼ cup (300 ml) water

*To **garnish**:*
Sprigs of fresh parsley

What you do

1 **Dry-fry** the almonds until they are lightly browned. Pour them onto a plate.

2 Lay the pork fillet on a board. Cut a slit from one end to the other. (If the fillet is in two pieces, cut a slit in each.)

3 Scatter the almonds over the pork and bring the two edges together. Knot the fillet together with string, making each knot about 2 in. (5 cm) apart.

4 **Peel** and **chop** the onion.

5 Heat the oil in a deep frying pan. Add the fillet and **fry** for 2–3 minutes on each side, until it is lightly browned.

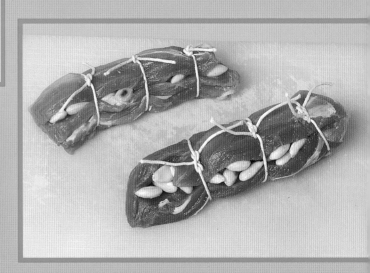

(!) **6** Add the onion and fry over medium heat for 3 minutes.

7 Put the sherry vinegar and 1¼ cup (300 ml) hot water into a small bowl. Crumble the stock cube into the liquid and stir well.

(!) **8** Add the liquid to the pan, bring to a **boil**, **cover**, and **simmer** for 1 hour.

(!) **9** Carefully lift the meat out of the pan and snip off the string. Cut the meat into thick **slices** and arrange on a plate.

10 Stir the cornstarch and cream together in a bowl. Add the cooking juices from the meat.

11 Pour the mixture back into the pan. **Reheat** for 2 minutes, stirring all the time. Pour over the pork and serve, garnished with parsley.

Potato and Onion Omelette

In Spain, this vegetable omelette is called a *tortilla* (pronounced *Tor-TEE-ya*). Spanish people serve it hot or cold in wedges, as a snack or part of a picnic. It makes a perfect snack or light lunch.

What you need

2 small potatoes
1 onion
4 eggs
1 tbsp olive oil
2 tbsp water

To garnish:
1 tomato

What you do

1 Wash and **peel** the potatoes.

2 Cut a ½-in. (1-cm) **slice** off the side of each potato and stand it flat on a board. Cut it into ½-in. (1-cm) wide slices, and then chop it into cubes.

3 Peel and slice the onion thinly.

4 Crack the eggs into a bowl. Add 2 tbsp cold water, and some salt and pepper. **Beat** them lightly with a fork.

5 Heat the oil in a large non-stick frying pan. Add the potatoes and **fry** over low-medium heat for 4 minutes, or until potatoes are soft.

6 Add the onion and cook for 10 minutes on medium heat, stirring occasionally.

7 Increase the heat a little under the frying pan. Pour the beaten eggs over the potato and onion mixture and cook for 4–5 minutes.

8 Cook until the eggs have set, and are starting to brown.

9 Slide a spatula around the edges of the *tortilla*. Hold the pan just above one side of a dinner plate, and slide the *tortilla* on to the plate.

10 Cut the tomato into wedges. Cut the *tortilla* into wedges, and serve hot or cold, garnished with the tomato.

SPANISH OMELETTE

When cooks add potatoes, onions, peas, slices of pepper, green beans, asparagus, mushrooms, or ham to an omelette, they are making a dish known in many countries as a Spanish omelette. It is an ideal way to use up leftover vegetables.

Roasted Vegetable Salad

In Spain, people eat this salad as a main dish, using chunks of crusty bread as a scoop, instead of knives and forks. It makes an ideal starter or side dish, too.

What you need

1 onion
1 green pepper
1 yellow pepper
1 red pepper
2 tbsp olive oil for
  brushing peppers

*For the garlic **dressing**:*
4 cloves garlic
½ tsp **ground** cumin
4 tbsp olive oil
1 lemon

What you do

1 **Preheat** the oven to 375°F (190°C).

2 Wrap the onion in foil, put it onto a baking sheet and **bake** for 15 minutes.

3 Brush the peppers with oil.

4 Arrange the peppers and garlic around the onion. Put back in the oven for 20 minutes. Put the hot peppers into a container and cover them.

5 When it is cool, take the foil off the onion, **peel** off its skin, and cut the flesh into thin strips.

6 Peel the skin off the peppers. Cut them in half, then into thin strips, throwing away the seeds and stalk. Arrange them on a plate.

7 Cut the end off each clove of garlic. Squeeze the flesh inside into a small bowl and squash it with a spoon to make a paste.

8 Cut the lemon in half. Use a lemon squeezer to squeeze out the juice.

9 Add the cumin, olive oil, lemon juice, and salt and pepper to the garlic paste.

10 Spoon the garlic dressing over the vegetables and serve.

White Bean and Pork Stew

Traditionally, miners working deep inside the mountains of northern Spain ate this filling stew, which is called *fabada*.

What you need

12 oz (350 g) dried white beans
1 lb (500 g) piece smoked ham
4 oz (100 g) belly pork (optional)
7 oz (200 g) pork sausages
7 oz (200 g) chorizo sausages
3 saffron strands
16 cups (4 l) water
Freshly-**ground** black pepper

What you do

1 Put beans and ham into separate large bowls. Cover both with 8 cups (2 l) of cold water. Leave overnight in the refrigerator.

2 If using belly pork, cut off the dark rind.

3 **Drain** the beans into a colander and put them into a large saucepan. Add the belly pork, sausages, chorizo, and ham. Cover with cold water. Bring to a **boil**, and boil for 10 minutes.

! **4** Using a slotted spoon, carefully skim any white froth off the boiling liquid.

5 Add the saffron, **cover**, and **simmer** for 1½ hours, stirring occasionally. Add more water to keep the beans covered if you need to.

! **6** Take the pan off the heat. Using a slotted spoon, lift the pieces of meat onto a chopping board. Cut them into bite-sized pieces.

7 Put the meat back into the pan and **reheat** thoroughly.

8 Add some freshly-ground black pepper, and serve in bowls with crusty bread.

Cod Croquettes

Croquettes are a popular **tapa** (see box on page 17), or side dish, all over Spain. They are made by mixing mashed potato or thick white sauce with fish, ham, or cheese, and rolling them into a sausage shape. Then they are **coated** in bread crumbs and **fried.**

What you need

1 lb (500 g) cod fillet
   (or any white fish)
2 cups (480 ml) milk
1 onion
5 tbsp olive oil
5 tbsp cornstarch
Ground black pepper
1 tbsp fresh dill
1 tbsp plain flour
2 eggs
6 oz (170 g) white
   bread crumbs

*To **garnish**:*
Sprigs of fresh dill
Wedges of lemon

What you do

(!) 1 Put the fish into a saucepan. Add the milk, **cover** and bring to a **boil.**

2 **Simmer** for 3 minutes, then leave to cool.

3 Using a spatula, lift the fish onto a plate. **Flake** it with a fork, throwing away any skin or bones.

4 Pour the cooking liquid into a measuring cup. Add cold water until the combined liquids equal 2 cups.

5 **Peel** the onion and **chop** it finely.

(!) 6 Heat 1 tbsp of the oil in the saucepan and **fry** the onion over a medium heat for 3 minutes.

7 In a bowl, stir 6 tbsp of the cooking liquid into the cornstarch to make a smooth paste.

8 Stir in the rest of the cooking liquid. Pour it over the onions and cook, stirring all the time, until the liquid thickens.

9 Chop the dill finely. Add it to the onions with the fish and some black pepper. Leave to cool for 1 hour. **Chill** for at least 2 hours.

10 Sprinkle flour over a work surface. Roll 3 tbsp of the chilled mixture into a sausage shape 3–4 in. (8–10 cm) long. Repeat until all the mixture is used.

11 **Beat** the eggs and pour them into a shallow bowl. Put the bread crumbs on a plate.

12 Dip the sausage shapes into the egg, and then roll them in the breadcrumbs.

⚠ 13 Heat the rest of the oil in a frying pan over medium heat. Fry the croquettes for 5 minutes, turning occasionally.

14 Serve garnished with sprigs of dill and lemon wedges.

Artichokes with Garlic Mayonnaise

Artichokes, known as *alcachofas* in Spanish, were first introduced to Spain by the Moors (see page 5). They are only available in Spain for a short period each year. To eat them Spanish-style, peel off a leaf, dip it into the garlic mayonnaise, and scrape the flesh off with your teeth.

What you need

4 globe artichokes
Pinch of salt
2 tbsp lemon juice

For the garlic mayonnaise:
1 cup (240 ml) ready-made mayonnaise
4 cloves of garlic

What you do

1 Twist or cut the stalks off the artichokes. Snip the pointed ends off the leaves with kitchen scissors.

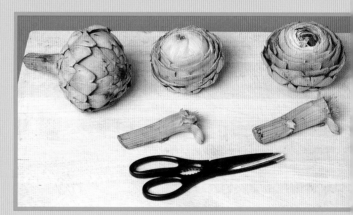

2 Put the artichokes into cold water with a pinch of salt.

3 Cut a lemon in half and squeeze out the juice with a lemon squeezer.

(!) 4 Bring a large pan of water to a **boil.** Add 2 tbsp of the lemon juice.

(!) 5 Using a slotted spoon, lower the artichokes into the pan, one at a time.

6 Bring back to a boil. **Cover** and **simmer** for 40 minutes.

7 **Peel** and crush the garlic. Stir it into the mayonnaise.

8 Lift the artichokes out of the pan with a slotted spoon. **Drain** them upside down in a colander until cool enough to handle.

9 Twist off the leaves in the middle of each artichoke. Scoop out the hairy pieces in the center with a spoon.

10 Put the leaves you took from the middle back into each artichoke, and serve warm or cold with the garlic mayonnaise.

Red Pepper Salad

This dish is known as *Ensalada de pimientos asados* in Spanish. It a speciality of the Rioja region of northern Spain, which is famous for its red wines. When the farmers prune the vines after the grape harvest, they pile the twigs to create big bonfires. Traditionally, local people roast peppers in the hot embers and make them into salads like this one.

What you need

4 red peppers
2 yellow peppers
2 cloves garlic
1 large beefsteak tomato
    or 3 medium tomatoes
3 tbsp olive oil
2 tsp sherry vinegar or
    white wine vinegar

What you do

1 **Preheat** the oven to 375°F (190°C).

2 Put the peppers, garlic, and tomato (or tomatoes) on a baking tray in the oven for 10 minutes.

3 Take the garlic and tomato (or tomatoes) off the tray, and leave the peppers to cook for an extra 10 minutes.

4 Cut the tomato (or tomatoes) into several pieces, and put them into a large sieve. Using the back of a spoon, push the tomato flesh and juice through the sieve. Throw away the skin and seeds.

5 Cut the end off the garlic and squeeze out the soft flesh. Stir into the tomato mixture.

6 Put the peppers into a container with a lid on. Leave them to cool.

7 **Peel** the skin from the peppers and cut them in half. Cut off the stalks, scoop out the seeds, and throw the stalks and seeds away.

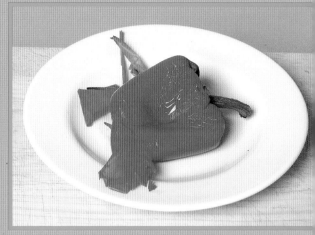

8 Cut the peppers into thin strips and arrange them on a plate.

9 Stir the oil and vinegar, and some salt and pepper, into the tomato mixture.

10 Spoon over the peppers and serve.

Nut Sweets

These soft sweets are called *turron* (pronounced *tu-RON*) in Spain. This *turron* recipe was first made in a village called Jijona in Alicante, a part of Spain famous for its almond trees.

What you need

1 sheet rice paper
4 oz (100 g) blanched almonds
3 oz (75 g) blanched hazelnuts
2 egg whites
3 oz (75 g) granulated sugar
4 tbsp honey
1 tsp ground cinnamon

What you do

1 Cover a baking tray with a sheet of rice paper.

2 **Dry-fry** the almonds and hazelnuts in a frying pan until pale brown. Pour them on a plate to cool.

3 Put the almonds and hazelnuts into a blender. **Blend** until they are finely **ground**.

4 To separate the egg yolks from the whites, carefully crack the egg. Keeping the yolk in one half of the shell, let the white drip into a bowl. Pass the yolk from one half of the shell to the other until all the white has dripped out. Put the yolk in a separate bowl. Do this for both eggs. (If there is any yolk in the white, use a spoon to scoop it out.)

5 Using an electric whisk, **whisk** the egg whites until they are frothy and firm.

6 **Fold** in the nuts with a metal spoon.

(!) **7** Put the sugar and honey into a non-stick saucepan. Heat them gently until the sugar **dissolves.** Bring the liquid to a **boil** and add the nut mixture.

8 Cook over low heat for 5 minutes, stirring all the time.

9 Spoon onto the rice paper and shape into a square about 1-in. (2½-cm) deep and 10-in. (25-cm) wide. Leave to cool.

10 Lift the *turron* onto a board. Sprinkle it with cinnamon. Cut it into 1-in. (2½-cm) squares.

Torrijas (Sugary Egg-Fried Bread)

Torrijas (pronounced *tor-EE-has*) are a favorite snack in Spain. They are simple to make and an ideal way of using up stale bread. If you want to be traditional, serve with a bowl of milk to dip the *torrijas* into.

What you need

1 cup (240 ml) milk
½ tsp **ground** cinnamon
3 tbsp superfine granulated sugar
8 slices of French bread, 1-in. (2½-cm) thick
2 eggs
2 tbsp olive oil
Extra ½ tsp ground cinnamon

What you do

(!) 1 Put the milk, cinnamon, and 2 tbsp sugar into a small saucepan. Bring to a **boil**. Turn off the heat and leave to cool for 5 minutes.

2 Arrange the bread slices in a shallow dish.

3 Pour the milk over the bread and leave for 10 minutes.

4 Lightly **beat** the eggs. Pour them into a shallow bowl.

5 Dip the bread slices into the beaten eggs to **coat** both sides.

(!) 6 Heat 1 tbsp of the oil in a frying pan until it is hot, but not smoking. Using a spatula, place two or three bread slices into the pan.

(!) 7 Fry over medium to low heat for 2 minutes, until the underside is starting to brown. Use the spatula to turn the bread over, and cook the other side.

8 Put the cooked bread slices onto a wire rack. Add the rest of the oil to the pan and cook the remaining bread slices.

9 Mix 1 tbsp sugar and the extra cinnamon together. Sprinkle them over the warm bread and serve immediately.

Magdalenas (Olive Oil Cakes)

For hundreds of years, the Spanish ate *magdalenas* (pronounced *mag-da-LAY-nas*) only on special holidays. Today, they eat them often, at breakfast and as an afternoon snack. Traditionally, cooks add olive oil to the recipe, and **bake** each little cake in a specially-shaped tin. However, you can make them just as well in muffin cups.

What you need

1 cup (100 g) self-rising flour

2 oz (50 g) superfine granulated sugar

1 lemon

½ cup (100 ml) olive oil

1 tbsp milk

3 eggs

1 tsp confectioners' sugar

What you do

1 **Preheat** the oven to 375°F (190°C).

2 Put the muffin cups into a baking tin for making 12 small cakes.

3 **Sift** the flour and sugar into a bowl.

4 **Grate** the lemon rind over a plate, using the fine side of the grater. Add the grated lemon rind to the flour and sugar.

5 Measure the oil into a measuring cup, and add the milk.

6 To separate the egg yolks from the whites, carefully crack the egg. Keeping the yolk in one half of the shell, let the white drip into a bowl. Pass the yolk from one half of the shell to the other until all the white has dripped out. Add the yolk to the oil and milk. Do this for both eggs. (If there is any yolk in the white, use a spoon to scoop it out and discard.)

7 Use an electric whisk to **whisk** the egg whites until they are frothy and firm.

8 Mix the oil, milk, and egg yolk mixture into the flour. Add half of the egg whites. Gently **fold** them into the flour mixture using a large metal spoon. Fold in the rest of the egg whites.

9 Spoon the mixture into the paper cases. **Bake** for 8–10 minutes, until the cakes are risen and golden.

10 Cool on a wire rack. **Dust** with icing sugar (see page 43) and serve.

Walnut Puffs

These puff-pastry squares are a popular Christmas treat in the Asturias region of northern Spain. Many farmhouses there have walnut trees in their gardens, and people use the nuts in their cooking.

What you need

2 tsp plain flour
6 oz (175 g) packet ready-made puff pastry
1½ (40 g) walnut pieces
1 tbsp confectioners' sugar
1 tbsp honey
1 egg
1 tsp confectioners' sugar for **dusting**

What you do

1 Sprinkle the flour over a work surface. Roll the pastry into a square about 10 in. (25 cm) wide. Trim any rough edges.

2 Cut the pastry into four strips, each 2 in. (5 cm) wide. Cut these in half to make eight rectangles 2 in. (5 cm) wide and 5 in. (13 cm) long.

3 **Chill** the pastry in the refrigerator.

4 Meanwhile, **blend** the walnut pieces in a blender until finely **chopped**.

5 Stir the nuts, sugar, and honey in a bowl.

6 **Preheat** the oven to 425°F (210°C). Brush the edges of the pastry with a little water.

7 Put 1 tsp of the walnut mixture at one end of each pastry rectangle, leaving a rim of pastry around the edge.

8 Fold the pastry over to make a square.

9 Press down the edges with the back of a fork. Put the squares onto a baking tray.

10 **Beat** the egg in a bowl with a fork. Brush some egg over the pastry.

⚠ **11** **Bake** the puffs on the top shelf of the oven for 8–10 minutes, until golden. Place on a wire rack to cool.

12 Dust with confectioners' sugar (see below). Serve warm or cold.

DUSTING

To add the finishing touch to cakes, spoon 1 tsp of confectioners' sugar into a sieve. Hold the sieve over the cake and lightly tap the side with the spoon. This is called dusting.

Further Information

Here are some places to find out more about Spain and Spanish cooking.

Cookbooks

Braman, Arlette N. *Kids Around the World Cook!* New York: John Wiley & Sons, 2000.

Pratt, Dianne. *Hey Kids, You're Cookin' Now*. Chattanooga: Harvest Hill Press, 1998.

Vezza, Diane Simone. *Passport on a Plate*. New York: Simon & Schuster, 1997.

Wilkes, Angela. *Children's Step-by-Step Cookbook*. New York, DK Publishing, 2001.

Books About Spain

Bader, Phillip and Patricia Moritz. *Spain*. Vero Beach, Fla.: The Rourke Book Company, Inc., 2002.

Costain, Meredith and Paul Collins. *Welcome to Spain*. Broomall, Penn.: Chelsea House Publishers, 2001.

Grinsted, Katherine. *Spain*. Milwaukee: Gareth Stevens, 1999.

Lior, Noa. *Spain the Land*. New York: Crabtree Publishing, 2001.

Rogers, Lura. *Spain*. Danbury, Conn.: Children's Press, 2001.

Measurements and Conversions

3 teaspoons=1 tablespoon	1 tablespoon=½ fluid ounce	1 teaspoon=5 milliliters
4 tablespoons=¼ cup	1 cup=8 fluid ounces	1 tablespoon=15 milliliters
5 tablespoons=⅓ cup	1 cup=½ pint	1 cup=240 milliliters
8 tablespoons=½ cup	2 cups=1 pint	1 quart=1 liter
10 tablespoons=⅔ cup	4 cups=1 quart	1 ounce=28 grams
12 tablespoons=¾ cup	2 pints=1 quart	1 pound=454 grams
16 tablespoons=1 cup	4 quarts=1 gallon	

Healthy Eating

This diagram shows which foods you should eat to stay healthy. Most of your food should come from the bottom of the food pyramid. Eat some of the foods from the middle everyday. Only eat a little of the foods from the top.

Healthy eating, Spanish-style

Spanish food varies a great deal. Some dishes are served with rice, others with potatoes or bread. Many recipes use a lot of vegetables from the middle layer of this pyramid, cooking them without much fat or oil. The Spanish eat a lot of fruits and fish, because both are plentiful. People in Spain enjoy cakes, but they tend to be small, eaten as a taste of something sweet after a main meal.

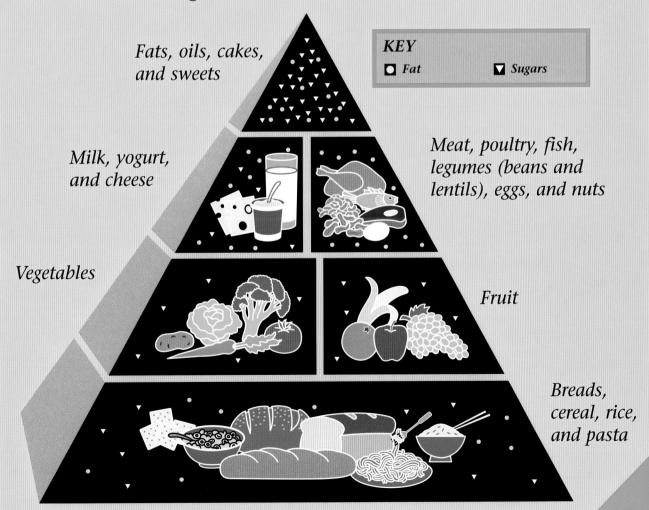

Fats, oils, cakes, and sweets

KEY
◻ *Fat*   ▽ *Sugars*

Milk, yogurt, and cheese

Meat, poultry, fish, legumes (beans and lentils), eggs, and nuts

Vegetables

Fruit

Breads, cereal, rice, and pasta

Glossary

bake cook something in the oven

beat mix ingredients together, using a fork or whisk

blend mix ingredients together in a blender or food processor

boil cook a liquid on the stove. Boiling liquid bubbles and steams.

broil cook under the broiler in the oven

chill put a dish in the refrigerator for a while before serving

chop cut into pieces using a sharp knife

coat cover with a sauce or batter

conquistador explorer sent from Spain to find and conquer new lands

cover put a lid on a pan, or put foil or plastic wrap over a dish

cured food, usually cooked meat, that is specially dried and flavored

defrost allow something that is frozen to thaw

dissolve mix something into a liquid until it disappears

drain remove liquid, usually by pouring something into a colander or sieve

dressing sauce for a salad

dry-fry cook over a high heat without any oil

dust sprinkle with confectioners' sugar or flour

export sell a product to another country

fertile land on which crops grow well

flake break fish into flakes with a fork

fold mixing wet and dry ingredients by making cutting movements with a metal spoon

fry cook something in oil in a pan

garnish decorate food, for example, with fresh herbs

grate break something, such as cheese, into small pieces using a grater

ground made into a fine powder

peel remove the skin of a fruit or vegetable

preheat turn on the oven in advance, so it is hot when you are ready to use it

reheat heat food thoroughly again

sift remove lumps from dry ingredients, such as flour, with a sieve

simmer cook liquid on the stove. Simmering liquid bubbles and steams gently.

skewer long wooden stick for holding food

slice cut something into thin, flat pieces

stir-fry cook foods in a little oil over a high heat, stirring all the time

tapa small dish of Spanish food, often served with a selection of others

tongs u-shaped kitchen utensil used for turning over hot food

whisk mix ingredients using a wire whisk

Index